F1RST

Day of School

A Book about Rules and Behavior

How do I get good grades in our class?

What are three **safety rules** for the playground?

What can I do to **help** someone who is hurt?

Why do we **raise our hand** in class?

Why do we stand in line?

How do we make a NEW STUDENT feel welcome?

What are we allowed to bring for **LUNCH**?

What should I do if the **electricity** goes out?

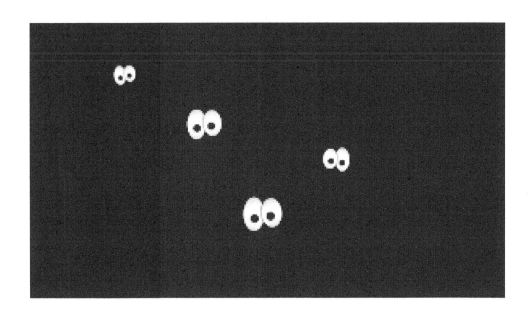

What are we allowed to WEAR to school?

Where are we allowed to RUN at school?

What if I really need to use the **RESTROOM** in the middle of class?

When is it okay to LAUGH?

What will happen if I forget my <u>homework</u>?

What are three rules about **PENCILS**?

How does <u>reading</u> improve my
IMAGINATION and CREATIVITY?

What will happen if I am *LATE* to school?

How can I help keep the classroom <u>clean</u> and <u>organized</u>?

What should I do if I feel like I am going to **throw up**?

What do I already know about measuring?

Will we **CELEBRATE** <u>birthdays</u> or <u>holidays</u> at school?

What should I do if there is a FIRE?

What should I do if I see TRASH on the ground?

What do I already know about vowels?

Do we get to DANCE in class?

What do I already know about RESPECT?

How do we keep others from getting SICK?

Do we get to write **POEMS** this year?

What should I do if I <u>break</u> my pencil?

Will I get to read a whole **BOOK** this year?

What are three rules about **PAPER**?

Do we get to write a **LETTER** this year?

Are we allowed to bring <u>toys</u> from home?

What do I do when I find something on the floor that isn't mine?

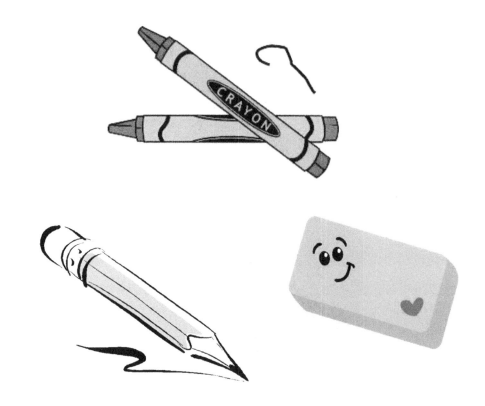

Why should we <u>obey</u> adults?

Do we get to write a **STORY** this year?

Is it okay to stick out your tongue at someone?

Why do kids like to **laugh**?

When should I be QUIET?

What can I do to make my friend SMILE?

What should I do if there is a tornado?

Will we get to work on **computers** this year?

When is it okay to CRY?

What do I do if I
don't know the answer
to a question?

Connecticut

DNT KWT

Constitution State

What are three rules about playing with a BALL at school?

How does <u>reading</u> make me smarter?

What are three things I can do to show that I am a good friend?

What do we already know about books?

What do we already know about addition and subtraction?

What **AWARDS** can I win this year?

What are three ways to show respect for a **BOOK**?

What should I do if my **pencil** is too small to fit into a pencil sharpener?

What are the school's rules about cell phones and cameras?

Do we get to go on a **FIELD TRIP** this year?

What are the school's rules about chewing gum?

What should I do when the teacher sends a NOTE to my parents?

What should I do if I hear two students arguing?

What do we do to help a substitute teacher?

What do we already know about spelling?

Why am I NOT allowed to <u>yell</u> at another kid?

What should I do if there is an earthquake?

When is it a good time to talk with my friends?

What do we already know about English?

How can I keep my desk clean and organized?

What do we already know about fractions?

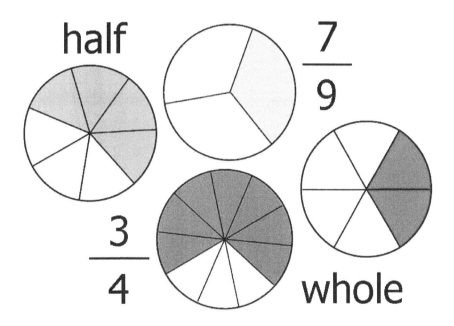

Name three **polite** things I can do at school.

What do we already know about the Earth?

What should I do if I hear the **fire drill**?

Do we get to **sing** in class?

What should I do if I see two students <u>fighting</u>?

Do we get to paint or draw in class?

What are three rules for riding on a bus?

What do we already know about multiplication and division?

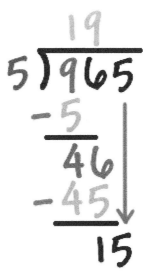

Do we get to solve puzzles in class?

Do you prefer to **shake hands** or to give someone a **high-five**?

What are three rules about **CRAYONS**?

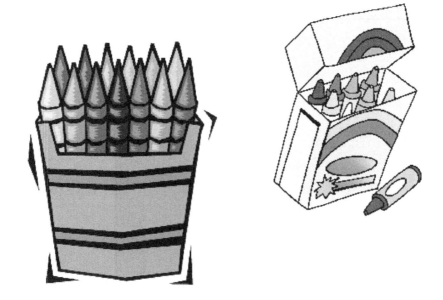

What do I do with the <u>pencil shavings</u> after I sharpen my pencil?

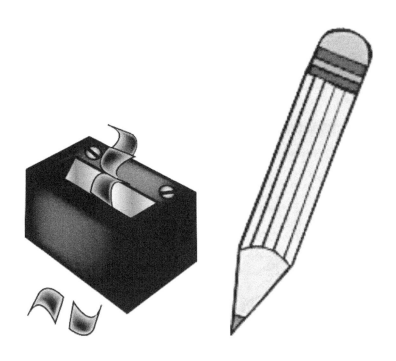

Do we get to play a **musical instrument** this year?

How does school make me a faster person with my BODY and with my MIND?

Does the teacher know the **answer** to every question?

What can I do to <u>help</u> someone who is in a bad mood?

What do we already know about **magnets**?

What do we already know about money?

What do I do if someone has something that is mine?

What do we already know about geometry?

What are three rules about **PENCILS**?

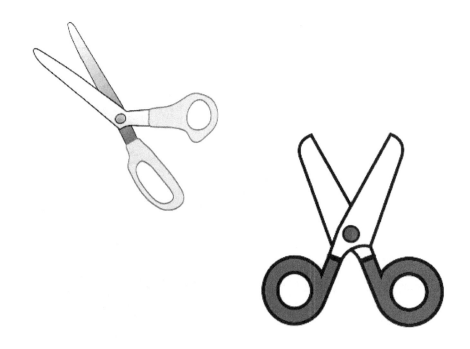

What happens if a <u>dragon</u> lands on the playground at recess?

When have you seen an <u>adult</u> reading a book?

How does school make me a **happier** person?

What do we already know about sign language?

What can I do to <u>help</u> someone who is ANGRY?

What do we already know about Spanish?

What can I do to <u>help</u> someone who is SAD?

What do we do if someone asks us if they can play with us?

What do we already know about multiplication and division?

Are we allowed to play **Tag** at recess?

Do we get to build stuff in class?

Do we get to learn about other cultures this year?

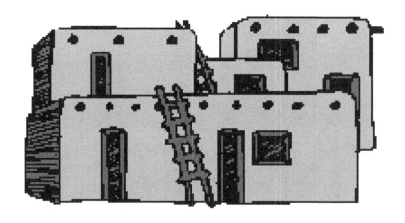

Why do we take **TESTS** at school?

Why is <u>sleep</u> important?

What do we already know about <u>comparing</u>?

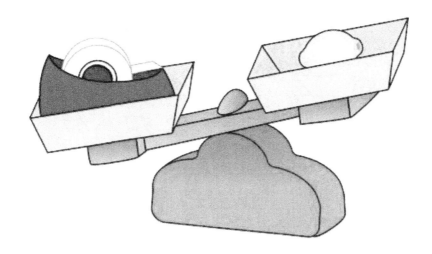

Who is in charge of our school?

What should I do if I see a dog on campus?

What are the school's rules on **hugging** my best friend?

What if a **monster** follows me to school?

What are three rules about backpacks?

Do <u>glasses</u> make a person smarter?

Why do kids like to **play games**?

How does school make me a **stronger** person in my BODY and in my MIND?

How does school make me a **nicer** person?

What must I do in order to graduate?

What FUN STUFF will we do this year?

The End

Made in the USA
Las Vegas, NV
09 August 2022